Zac
Efron

Zac Efron

by Terri Dougherty

LUCENT BOOKS

An imprint of Thomson Gale, a part of The Thomson Corporation

THOMSON

GALE

™

Detroit • New York • San Francisco • New Haven, Conn. • Waterville, Maine • London

© 2008 Thomson Gale, a part of The Thomson Corporation.

Thomson and Star Logo are trademarks and Gale and Lucent Books are registered trademarks used herein under license.

For more information, contact:
Lucent Books
27500 Drake Rd.
Farmington Hills, MI 48331-3535
Or you can visit our Internet site at http://www.gale.com

LIBRARY OF CONGRESS CATALOGING-IN-PUBLICATION DATA

Dougherty, Terri.
  Zac Efron / by Terri Dougherty.
    p. cm. — (People in the news)
  Includes bibliographical references and index.
  ISBN-13: 978-1-4205-0017-2
  1. Efron, Zac—Juvenile literature. 2. Actors—United States—Biography—Juvenile literature. I. Title.
  PN2287.E395D68 2008
  792.02'8092--dc22
  [B]
                                                                2007032102

ISBN-10: 1-4205-0017-1

Printed in the United States of America

Contents

Fame and celebrity are fascinating. We are drawn toward people who walk in fame's spotlight, whether they are known for great achievements or for famous acts. The lives of celebrities attract attention, perhaps because their experiences seem in some ways so different from, yet in other ways so similar to, our own.

Newspapers, magazines, and television regularly take advantage of our fascination by running profiles of famous people. For example, television programs such as *Entertainment Tonight* devote all their programming to stories about entertainment and entertainers. Magazines such as *People* fill their pages with stories of the private lives of famous people. Even newspapers, newsmagazines, and television news frequently look at the lives of well-known personalities. But despite the number of articles and programs on offer, few provide us with more than a superficial glimpse of celebrity life.

Lucent's People in the News series offers young readers a closer look at the lives of today's newsmakers, the influences that have shaped them, and the impact they have had on the world, and on other people's lives. The subjects of the series come from many disciplines and walks of life. They include authors, musicians, athletes, political leaders, entertainers, entrepreneurs, and others who have made a mark on modern life and who, in many cases, will continue to do so for years to come.

These biographies are more than just factual accounts. Each book emphasizes the contributions, achievements, or deeds that have brought fame to the individual. The books also show how that person has influenced modern life. Authors describe their subjects in a realistic, unsentimental light. For example, Bill Gates—the cofounder and chief executive officer of the software giant Microsoft—has made personal computers the most vital tool of the modern age. Few dispute his business skills, his perseverance, or his technical expertise, but critics say he is ruthless in his dealings with competitors and is driven more by his desire to maintain Microsoft's dominance in the computer industry than by an interest in furthering technology.

In these books, young readers will encounter inspiring stories about real people who have achieved success despite enormous obstacles. Oprah Winfrey—the most powerful, most watched, and wealthiest woman on television today—spent the first six years of her life in the care of her grandparents while her unwed mother sought work and a better life elsewhere. Her adolescence was colored by promiscuity, pregnancy at age fourteen, rape, and sexual abuse.

Each author documents and supports his or her work with a selection of primary and secondary source quotations taken from diaries, letters, speeches, and interviews. All quotes are footnoted to show readers exactly how and where biographers got their information, and provide guidance for further research. The quotations bring the text to life by giving readers eyewitness accounts of the life and achievements of each person covered in the People in the News series.

In addition, each book in the series includes photographs, annotated bibliographies, timelines, and comprehensive indexes. For both the casual reader and the student researcher, the People in the News series offers an insight into the lives of today's newsmakers—people who shape the way we live, work, and play in the modern age.

Musical Star

Zac Efron thought he was just making a little musical. There had been a few weeks of rehearsals, a month of filming, and then a waiting period while the movie was edited. It had taken less than two months of his life and would be another small step in the acting career he had been working on since he was eleven.

Not that making the movie was easy. The audition itself had taken more than seven hours. Then came some exhausting hours of learning lines, dance moves, and enough basketball skills to make it look like he owned the court. Zac had stretched his skills to include athletic moves he wasn't comfortable with before, and he had danced until his body was sore. Hard work, to be sure, but the movie was not even going to end up in theaters—it was a made-for-television show for the Disney Channel.

The buzz, however, started to grow even before the musical premiered. Videos and catchy songs caught the interest of tweens and teens. When *High School Musical* finally made its appearance on January 20, 2006, it was the beginning of a new craze. The movie, the soundtrack, and the young actors in the film were all brought to the public's attention. Zac's fame rose with the movie's popularity, and suddenly opportunities and offers he could only have dreamed of were coming his way.

Zac was no newcomer to musicals or acting, and he knew the hard work that went into landing a role. Zac had been doing community theater since age eleven. After many auditions he had landed a few guest roles in television shows and had been chosen for the lead part in a minor movie. Zac was also part of a television series for a time; before *Musical* his biggest acting job had been a character on the show *Summerland*.

Zac Efron's fame rose with the success of **High School Musical.**

Thanks to his role on *Summerland*, Zac had attracted a small following. His fans were mainly young girls who appreciated the young star's good looks. However, Zac's popularity was in danger of fading when *Summerland* was cancelled after two seasons. Zac had made a few movies, and he had earned some respect from his costars, but he did not stand out significantly from other brown-haired young actors when he auditioned for roles.

High School Musical changed all that. A number of fans began to appreciate Zac's looks and talent, and directors now recognized him when he tried out for a part. His face appeared on teen magazines, and he was named one of *People* magazine's 100 Most Beautiful. Suddenly, Zac was one of the most popular teenagers in America.

Zac used his newfound fame to build his career. He did not necessarily want to be pigeonholed into being a musical actor, but when he was offered a part in the musical *Hairspray* he did not turn it down. His rise to fame was questioned, however. As Zac's voice changed, singing became a challenge for him. While the other *High School Musical* actors got record deals after the movie's popular premiere, Zac had to admit that he had not done all of his singing in the film.

The issue faded when Zac did his own singing in *Hairspray*, a movie that helped to advance his career. The film was edgier than the squeaky clean *High School Musical* and rather than working with new teen stars, Zac was acting alongside veterans John Travolta and Michelle Pfeiffer. The young star worked on his singing and dancing skills to prove he was worthy of being cast in such a star-filled production.

Zac's popularity continued to move his career forward. Audition offers kept coming his way, and he postponed his college plans so he could concentrate on acting opportunities. There was a sequel to *High School Musical*, a pilot for a television show, and more movies to audition for.

Hairspray *helped to advance Zac's career.*

Zac was realistic about these opportunities and his career. His days as a teen idol could not go on forever, and he wanted to take advantage of his recent fame. He was already thinking ahead. Zac eventually wanted to go to college, major in film, and one day work behind the camera. *High School Musical* had given his career a jump start, but now it was up to him to make the most of the fame that came with it. Zac would have to make his choices wisely as he became used to being a star.

Chapter 1

He'd Rather Act

Growing up near the Pacific coast in Southern California, Zac Efron was a typical American kid. He collected autographed baseballs, went to the beach on sunny days, and got into disagreements with his younger brother. But Zac also had an interest that began to set him apart from his peers: he loved to act.

Acting roles in community theater productions sparked Zac's desire to perform onstage. As more roles came his way, he thought about taking his interest beyond his hometown and the community theater. Zac took steps toward beginning an acting career by getting an agent and going to lots of auditions.

California Guy

Zachary David Alexander Efron was born in San Luis Obispo, California, on October 18, 1987. His parents were David Efron and Starla Baskett, who had met at a power plant where they were both working. Zac had a brother, Dylan, who was four years younger than him.

Zac was raised in Arroyo Grande, near San Luis Obispo. The city of almost 17,000 people is midway between San Francisco and Los Angeles along California's coast. The city is known for its antique stores, wineries, and agriculture. It draws tourists to such local celebrations as the annual Strawberry Festival and the Harvest Festival. The region has a mild climate, with a few days of scorching heat or freezing temperatures each year.

The Efrons were not a Hollywood show business family. Zac's dad, David, was an electrical engineer and his mother worked at

Zac's parents, David and Starla, were always supportive of his acting and singing.

a power plant. Zac had a stable upbringing in a good community. For fun he shot baskets and played hacky sack in the driveway in front of his home.

Zac had a go at team sports as a kid, playing Little League baseball and basketball. However, he admits that he was no super athlete. "I was the worst kid on my 6th grade basketball team," he said. "I passed the ball to the wrong team and they scored

Puppy Time

When Zac was growing up, his family also included a pair of puppies. The Efrons owned two Australian Shepherds, affectionate medium-sized, long-haired dogs that were commonly used for herding. The family's dogs were named Dreamer and Puppy. In addition, the family had a Siamese cat named Simon.

at the buzzer in double over time to win the championship. Its one of those memories that STILL makes you squirm when you think about it."[1]

Finding His Voice

Sports may not have been Zac's strong point, but it became clear that he had another talent. Zac's parents heard him singing around the house and were surprised by the quality of his voice. "I used to sing the Tin Man song from 'The Wizard of Oz' at, like, three," he said. "As I got older, I sang my favorite songs from the radio. My parents thought I had a good voice and they encouraged me. They both love music."[2]

Zac enjoyed singing, so the next obvious step was to find a place where he could use his talent. After it became clear that team sports did not work out for Zac, his parents encouraged him to get involved in other activities. When his father saw that a local community theater was putting on the play *Gypsy*, he urged Zac to try out.

Zac, then eleven years old, was not excited about auditioning for the part. Although he was not an exceptional athlete, he still had dreams of playing professional sports one day, rather than acting onstage. However, his parents' wishes won him over and he went to the audition. Zac had a horrible time there. He was

Zac became a regular in local musical productions.

scared and was not at all excited about having an opportunity to act. However, something about him attracted the attention of the play's director. "It was a very small part, Newsboy No. 1," he said. "I was terrified going into this audition, but I went in and got the part."[3]

In the Stands

Zac was not athletic as a youngster, but that did not mean he did not enjoy sports. He was a fan of the San Francisco Giants baseball team and the Los Angeles Lakers basketball team. "Although I wanted to be a player when I was younger I was too small," he said. "It took me a long time before I actually started growing." When he was older, Zac played basketball for fun and also went to the gym to work out. In addition, he added to his love of sports by collecting autographed baseballs. Zac had autographs from many Giants players, although he did not get one from Barry Bonds.

"It's My Life: Zac Efron," PBSKidsGo! http://pbskids.org/itsmylife/celebs/interviews/zac.html.

A New Interest

Once Zac got the role, his attitude toward acting changed. As he began rehearsing and performing, he found that he loved acting and musical theater. Zac wanted to get better, and he took voice and piano lessons to improve his musical ability. He also watched musicals and loved it when the entire cast would break into song.

After the performances of *Gypsy* came to an end, Zac tried out for more shows. He no longer needed encouragement from his parents, and he became a regular at community theater auditions for productions at Unity Church and the Little Theater in San Luis Obispo. "From Day One, I got addicted to being on stage and getting the applause and laughter,"[4] he said.

More Musicals

Zac soon built a résumé of roles in local productions, including the lead role of Harold Hill in *The Music Man*. He also had roles

Musical Memory

Zac enjoyed watching musicals when he was a kid, and his favorite was *Singin' in the Rain*. He especially enjoyed the scene with Donald O'Connor singing *Make Them Laugh*. "I've watched it fifty times probably in one night, laughing harder every time," he said.

"It's My Life: Zac Efron," PBSKidsGo!, http://pbskids.org/itsmylife/celebs/interviews/zac.html.

in musicals such as *Peter Pan, Grease, Mame,* and *Little Shop of Horrors.* Being around other actors and vocal artists helped Zac to improve. "That's my roots," he said, "Songs and dance on small stages all across the central coast of California."[5]

Zac's parents were not the only ones who noticed his talent for acting. When he was in middle school, Zac's eighth-grade drama teacher suggested he take his talent to the next level by getting an agent. With an agent, he would be able to audition for television shows and movies. Zac took his teacher's advice and got an agent who could help him get called to auditions for television shows, commercials, and movies.

Auditions and Rejections

Taking his acting career to a new level meant that Zac would have to give more time to it. Zac and his mom made the three-hour drive from their home in Arroyo Grande to Los Angeles three days a week so he could go to auditions. Their trips often ended in disappointment. Although Zac's agent found him many opportunities to audition, the young teen got few roles. There was a lot of competition and Zac realized that the chance of landing a role was not great. "It's ruthless," Zac says. "There are several thousand kids out there with brown hair and blue

Give it a Try

When he was asked to give advice to kids who were interested in acting, Zac said the most important thing was to get out and get involved. Being involved in a school production or doing set decorating, acting, or lighting were all ways to participate. "Go out and try theater. Audition. Make your own path. If you're enjoying it, you'll get there."

There was no reason a person interested in acting should wait around, he said. "My advice would be to go and sign up for the first play you can find, audition and see how you like it. If you enjoy being on stage, then I can almost guarantee that you are going to like being in front of the camera."

Dallas Morning News, "Learning to be 'High School' stars," http://zacefronfan.org/press/learninghstars.php.

Emily Doveala, "The Scoop on 'High School Musical,'" *Time for Kids*, http://zacefronfan.org/press/scoophsm.php.

eyes that are my age trying to be in movies. Getting a job is like beating a casino."[6]

Zac had many hopeful callbacks, but just as many heartbreaking results. For some roles he tried out ten times only to be rejected at the end. Sometimes he would be told he had the role, only to find it eventually went to someone else. Despite knowing that it was unlikely that he would be chosen for a role, Zac persevered. He knew there was still a chance that an audition could be the one that got him the part. "For every role that I have done on TV and movies, I've auditioned for thirty or forty," he said.[7]

A Pro

Thanks to his persistence, Zac eventually landed some small roles. He added to his stage acting experience by taking guest parts in television shows. Zac was not a series regular, but even a small part was a step in the right direction for the young actor.

Zac's first professional part came in 2002. It was on the series *Firefly*, a science fiction and adventure series that appeared for a short time on the Fox television network. Zac played a young version of the show's Dr. Simon Tam character. The small role did not set him on his way to stardom, but it was nice to get a part after so many tries. Zac landed other small roles over the next few years, including in the hospital drama *ER* in 2003 and in the drama *The Guardian* in 2004.

Zac also had success in getting larger parts in television pilots. These shows were made by production companies in the hope that they would be bought by a network and given a regular timeslot on television. In 2003, Zac's career hit a new high when he landed a starring role in the television comedy *The Big, Wide World of Carl Laemke*. The show allowed Zac to be the central part of a series, but a network did not choose to buy the pilot. The same fate was in store for the next pilot Zac was part of, *Triple Play*, in 2004. Although the shows he was part of were not widely viewed, Zac was getting better at landing roles. Even though the roles were not bringing him fame and fortune, Zac was getting his first jobs as a professional actor.

Juggling Classes and Acting

While Zac was busy trying to find work as an actor, he was also going to high school. With all the traveling and auditioning he was doing, Zac did not have much time to hang out with his friends. The activities he did take part in outside of school involved singing, dancing, and theater. He often had to tell his friends he could not hang out with them because he had to go to play practice or an audition.

Zac said there was peer pressure to overcome because the other kids in school were not as enthusiastic about theater as he was. They could not understand why Zac would spend so much time trying to be an actor. However, his friends sometimes changed their minds after coming to watch the plays he appeared in. They would then understand why Zac was missing school and could not spend more time hanging out with them.

At the Circus

Zac's only family link to show business came through his grandmother. She had been in the circus at one time. Zac said her work there did not influence his decision to start an acting career, however.

Zac enjoyed school but never felt like he was part of the popular crowd. He had friends throughout the school but did not feel like he was part of any particular group. In addition to having a job that kept him from spending time with his classmates, Zac was going through an awkward stage. Early in high school, Zac was short and skinny and had a gap in his teeth. When he was older, he was known for his good looks, especially his eyes, but during his early years of high school he was teased about the way he looked. Zac got along with his classmates, but he had to deal with some unkind comments about his imperfect teeth. Zac's experiences in high school taught him the importance of following his own interests. "I was never the cool kid," he said. "There's a lot of peer pressure and you have to take everything you hear with a grain of salt and follow your instincts."[8]

Following His Own Path

While Zac had to sacrifice time with his friends for his acting career, he did not mind. It was his choice to continue with acting, and his many auditions were starting to pay off. Although Zac had been rejected for many roles, he had also won a few parts and had even been cast as a major character in television pilots.

None of Zac's roles led to fame just yet, but he was happy to continue to work at something he enjoyed. At a young age Zac found that team sports were not his thing, but acting held his interest. He was part of a cast rather than a member of a team.

Zac's interest in acting had its drawbacks. He was too busy with acting and auditions to take part in other high school activities, and the more energy and time he put into acting the less time he had to spend with his friends. But Zac learned to ignore negative comments and to follow his interests.

A series of small successes encouraged Zac to keep going. While he was in high school, his efforts began to pay off with some guest star roles and main parts in television pilots. He was not a star by any means, but he was doing what he liked to do.

Chapter 2

Teen Dream

Zac was not yet a well-known actor, but he did not give up. He wouldn't let disappointing auditions or failed television pilots keep him from trying again. Zac's efforts eventually paid off, when he was given a guest spot on the television series *Summerland* in 2004. This led to further appearances on the show and the first sign of becoming a professional actor.

It was not Zac's acting ability that attracted the most attention, however. Zac also began to be known for his looks, especially his eyes. Zac's role on *Summerland* brought his first taste of fame when girls started to make Web sites about him and put his picture on their walls.

Summerland

Summerland, on the WB Network, starred Lori Loughlin, who was best known for her role as Becky, the wife of Uncle Jesse, on the television series *Full House*. In *Summerland*, Loughlin played a fashion designer who lived in a beautiful California beach town and had to care for her sister's children. Also on the show was teen heartthrob and singer Jesse McCartney.

Zac was given the role of Cameron Bale, a teen who was crazy about girls. He was cast as a love interest for one of the characters, and his first scene for the show was an uncomfortable one. It called for him to kiss his costar, Kay Panabaker. Because Zac was new to the show and the people he was working with, the scene was not an easy one for him to film. But the rest of the cast made him feel comfortable on the set. "Those are really tough, but everyone

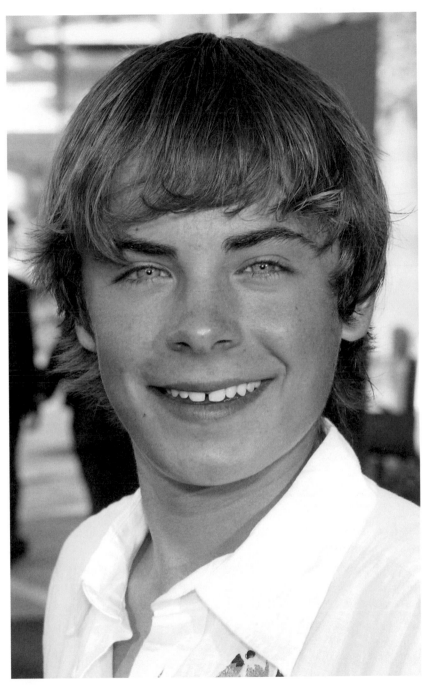

In the television series Summerland, Zac was a guest star at first but then became a regular.

First Kiss

When Zac was a fourteen-year-old on the show *Summerland* the script called for him to kiss his costar, actress Kay Panabaker. It was the first time she had ever kissed a boy and she was quite nervous. Zac told her she seemed mellow. He also said that he hoped he didn't ruin her first kiss. Kay assured him that he did not.

made me feel right at home," he said. "It was a blast because we got it out of the way. It made me feel like part of the cast."[9]

A Regular

By the next season, Zac felt even more at home on the set because he was made a permanent part of the *Summerland* cast. Until now, he had only had guest-starring roles, and becoming a series regular made him feel much more comfortable around the other actors. "…you don't really get to know the cast when you're there for just a day or two," he said. "Then when *Summerland* came along I was just a guest-star for a time but slowly I became part of the cast. Everything is completely different when you're around people that are like your family. And when you get to know everybody it's more like hanging around with a bunch of friends. It's much more relaxed."[10]

After Zac became a series regular, his character was given more depth. As his role expanded, Zac had to dig deeper to perform the part. Details of his character's life were brought out to reveal that he had an alcoholic father and had been abused. This made the role a difficult one for Zac, but it was a challenge that he was keen to take on. "Luckily, I've never had to deal with the kind of intense pain he's had to deal with," he said. "That makes it exciting for me. I really get into trying to imagine what it's like to be in someone else's shoes."[11]

Kay Panabaker played Zac's love interest on the television series Summerland.

Surf's Up

Being part of the *Summerland* cast introduced Zac to a new sport: he fell in love with surfing. He got a new surfboard and a wetsuit as a Christmas present, and he hit the waves. Zac claimed not to be afraid of sharks, saying that getting bit would make a person lucky because it would make a person a legend.

Being a series regular helped Zac improve his acting skills. The young actor was able to watch his costars and learn from them. He relaxed on the set and began to feel what it meant to have a steady job. He was no longer a guest star constantly auditioning, but an actor with a permanent role.

Move to L.A.

Getting the job as a regular cast member meant that Zac now spent much of his time in Los Angeles. The long commute from his home in Arroyo Grande soon became an issue. Zac could not afford to spend most of his day on the road, so he moved to Los Angeles after his role was expanded. His family still kept their Arroyo Grande home, however.

Living in Los Angeles meant Zac avoided the long commute, but it also meant that he had to leave his high school classmates behind. Rather than enroll in another high school in Los Angeles, Zac got his high school education from an on-set tutor. Zac had done well in his traditional high school classes, but he found it a challenge to juggle his school work and his acting commitments. Moving to Los Angeles and getting a tutor made life easier. Zac had tried to handle both traditional school and his acting career, but just handing in his homework became a chore. "It's difficult trying to go back and forth between work and school," he said.

"If I go down to L.A. to work, I miss a whole day of school. Then you're mailing all your school work back and forth to your teachers, and it gets complicated."[12]

Young Fans

Zac's role on *Summerland* took him away from his school and hometown and changed his life in other ways, too. The young actor now had fans, and the majority of them were young girls. The sixteen-year-old was becoming a teen heartthrob. Teen magazines realized that kids wanted to know more about him, and his picture appeared in *Popstar* magazine as well as on the cover of *Tiger Beat* and *Teen People*. Fans made Web sites about him, posted pictures of him online, and chatted about the young actor.

Despite the attention, Zac still felt like a normal teen. He saw himself as just an average kid who liked to play video games and sometimes fought with his brother. The attention he received from the television show seemed unreal to him. "It's really strange to type my name into Google and have more than twenty hits. It's a trip! People call me up and say 'Wow, you have a website' and I say 'which one?'"[13]

Zac did not mind the attention he was beginning to get from fans, however. He was still a kid himself and understood how other kids felt. When he had been younger, a poster of Tyra Banks hung on the ceiling above his bed, so he felt honored rather than offended when he thought about girls having his picture on their walls.

Too Popular

While Zac appreciated the attention, he soon learned that it had a down side. It was not only in magazines and on the Internet that Zac was getting noticed. With his face on television, in magazines, and posted on Web sites, it was only a matter of time before some fans began noticing Zac when he went out in public. While it was flattering when people recognized him as an actor, there were also times when it was annoying.

The recognition usually started quietly and built from there. When he went to the mall, a few young girls would start following Zac around. The crowd would slowly grow as he went from store to store and finally one person would say hello. Suddenly it would seem like the entire crowd was coming toward him. "One time I got trapped in a mall with a friend and we had to run to leave the place," he recalled.[14]

Acting, Not Singing

Zac was getting some recognition for his acting, but the work he was doing was quite different from the community theater plays he had done in the past. The majority of these had been musicals, but Zac's role in *Summerland* did not call for him to do any singing. A number of young actors tried to add to their popularity by starting a singing career as well. Zac hesitated to go down this road, however. He had taken voice lessons and knew he had a good singing voice, but he had not done any singing in public outside of musical theater.

At this time, Zac didn't want to take the route to the recording studio that so many young stars were making. He still liked to sing, but the roles that he was offered did not need it. At this point in his career he wanted to concentrate on acting. If he ever recorded a CD, he wanted to do it his way by creating his own music and writing his own songs. It was not something he was looking to do in the near future, however. "That's far, far away if I ever did consider it," he said.[15]

Zac had a costar who did make the move to a singing career. Jesse McCartney, the other teen heartthrob on *Summerland*, was also a singer, and Zac praised him for his vocal talent. "That guy has a great voice," Zac said.[16]

True Friends

Zac was supportive of Jesse's two careers. Some of Zac's old friends were also supportive of his career and excited that his role on *Summerland* was turning him from a typical teen into a

Jesse McCartney, Zac's co-star on Summerland, was also a singer.

budding star. Although Zac was now living in Los Angeles, he still managed to stay in touch with the friends he had grown up with. Zac admitted that not everyone he knew was happy about his success. Some kids were jealous and could not understand how he could have gotten a role in a television show. But although some people did not wish him well, Zac's true friends were supportive and happy for him. "Most of them are pretty darn good about it," he said. "They're cool. They're pretty supportive—the ones who don't become jealous and blinded by what it is. They're real friends—even though I see them less often, it's better than ever."[17]

Cancellation and a Movie

Zac's friends did not have the chance to see him on television for long, however. Zac soon realized that fame, and a television series, could soon end. He had become popular with young teens after getting a role on *Summerland*, but his fame was not enough to save the series. The show was cancelled in 2005. Zac appeared in sixteen episodes in 2004 and 2005, and the last show aired July 18, 2005.

Summerland was not the only job keeping Zac busy, however. He also got a major role in the television movie *Miracle Run*, which starred Mary-Louise Parker and Aidan Quinn as the parents of autistic twins. Zac and Thomas Lewis played the twins, who had a condition that made it difficult for them to interact socially.

This was Zac's first major movie role, and he wanted to do his best. To learn how to play the part of an autistic boy, he read up on the subject. He also drew on his experiences with a person he knew who showed characteristics similar to autism.

To pull off the role, Zac needed to act with the correct mannerisms, attitude, and speech patterns. It was a challenging part, but Zac did a good job and was nominated for a Young Artist Award for his role in the picture. Costar Quinn was impressed with both Zac and Thomas Lewis. "I was kind of amazed by the job they did," said Quinn, who has an autistic daughter. "In a

Getting to Know You

Even after *Summerland* was cancelled, Zac continued to be featured in magazines aimed at young teens. In an interview with Teen Magazine, he revealed a few little known facts about himself:

- The first thing he did every morning was sing in the shower.
- Watching the entire Rocky series got him hooked on fitness.
- His brother scared him by asking him to reach into a hole for a golf ball, and then screaming "snake!" Zac was so scared he almost passed out.
- The cereals in his cupboard included Kashi, Granola, Honey Nut Cheerios and Quaker Oats.
- His idea of Heaven on Earth was being first in line when Krispy Kreme donut samples were handed out.
- He makes macaroni and cheese when he has to cook dinner.
- When he was in sixth grade, he splurged on an electric scooter.

short period of time, they learned certain looks, ways of walking and holding their hands—things that are particular to autistic kids that, when you're the parent of an autistic child, you know inside and out."[18]

The Derby Stallion

Zac was steadily building his career and was receiving good reviews for his work. But he had yet to break out of the crowd—all his parts so far were in supporting roles.

All that changed, however, with the movie *The Derby Stallion*, a film Zac made while he was still part of the *Summerland* cast. Zac made the movie while the television show was taking a

The Derby Stallion *was Zac's first lead in a movie.*

break. Zac was immediately drawn to the *Derby Stallion* script. "The first time I read the script I knew it was going to be awesome," he said. "It was my first chance to be a lead in a movie. That's a big deal."[19]

The movie featured Bill Cobbs as a former Derby racer. Zac tried out for the part of Patrick McCardle, a boy who wanted to learn to ride and race. When he was auditioning for the role, Zac pictured Cobbs as the person giving him the guidance and wisdom he would need to be a successful rider. "[When] I found out he was doing it, I was like this is just amazing," he said. "It's all coming together."[20]

Horsing Around

After Zac got the role, he found that he had to learn some new skills. When he was offered the part, he thought that the horseback riding would be done by stuntmen. He soon found out differently. "Before *Derby Stallion* I had no experience on a horse, I had never actually been on one," he said. "Little did I know three lessons into the *Derby Stallion* experience I would be jumping horses. We were doing like three-foot jumps and doing sprints and all kinds of stuff."[21]

Zac had thought he would never be interested in riding, but his role in *The Derby Stallion* changed his mind. Learning to ride was painful at times, because he had sore muscles and fell from the horse. But he also found it a great deal of fun. By the time filming ended, Zac found horseback riding to be a thrilling experience.

Musician Billy Preston and soap opera star Tonja Walker were also part of the cast. Zac played a fifteen-year-old boy who was trying to figure out what to do with his life. His character made his parents let him work with misunderstood horse trainer Houston Jones, played by Cobbs. In addition to learning about the world of steeplechase racing and riding in the Derby Cup, Zac's character also dealt with a rich bully who wanted to defend his title as the Derby Cup champion.

The movie's plot also called for a romance to develop between Zac's character and Jill Overton, played by Crystal Hunt. Jill was the new girl in town, and she became friends with Patrick as they both tried to help Jones. As they got to know one another better, their friendship turned to romance. Once again, Zac's role called for him to kiss his costar.

Promoting the Film

Zac was proud of his work in *Derby Stallion*, but the movie was not released in theaters. The film made its Southern California premiere in April 2006 at the Newport Beach Film Festival. It was shown on television in Hungary and France but was not widely released in the United States until it came out on DVD in 2007. At that time, the film was promoted through its

Zac continued to audition for acting roles after **The Derby Stallion.** *He had his fans, but he was not instantly recognized by directors, so he had to work hard to prove himself.*

Web site. The DVD contained many extras that focused on Zac, including an interview and photo gallery. The DVD also came with photos of Zac, because it appealed to the young girls who were his fans.

Some reviewers criticized the movie for poor editing and a weak plot. "*The Derby Stallion* is actually a very bad movie," wrote David Cornelius on DVD Talk. "This one's riddled in lazy cliché and sloppy formula work. The direction is poor, the supporting cast is shaky, the sluggish pacing is aggravating."[22] Others thought the film was a fine family movie, which was certain to be a hit with Zac's fans. "This coming-of-age story is something kids can share with their parents," wrote Francine Brokaw on MovieWeb. "This is a cute story about this young boy's desire to do something different with his life."[23]

While he was making the movie, it was clear that Zac had become a heartthrob. Walsh, who played Zac's mother in the movie, said her daughters were quite taken with the young actor. "Oh my gosh—they just love Zac," she said.[24] Even Cornelius, although he did not like the movie, had to admit that Zac had talent. He called Zac a natural actor who was destined to move on to better things. "*The Derby Stallion* shows a solid young actor comfortable in front of the camera," he wrote. "Better, he's determined to make the most out of problematic material, and while we never believe the character, we believe Efron."[25]

Plugging Away

Although the movie was not a high-quality film, Zac's lead role in *The Derby Stallion* was another positive step in his young career. He was becoming a busy actor who continued to audition and was determined to find more acting work. While Zac had his fans, however, he was far from a household name. His role on *Summerland* had brought him recognition in stories in teen magazines and on the Internet, but he still faced an uphill battle when he went in to audition for roles.

Zac was not immediately recognized by directors and had to prove himself every time. He continued to deal with his share of rejection, but he did not stop trying. Zac had success in getting a few roles; in addition to the movies he made, he was in episodes of *CSI: Miami* and *NCIS*. He also made the television pilot *If You Lived Here, You'd Be Home Now.*

Then, not too long after *Summerland* was cancelled, Zac heard about another audition. This time it would take advantage of the singing and dancing he had done in so many community theater roles. When auditions for *High School Musical* opened up, Zac pressed his agent to get him an audition for one of the lead parts.

Chapter 3

Making *Musical*

Zac felt his background in community theater and his interest in musicals would make him right for the lead role of Troy Bolton in *High School Musical*. For the young actor, it looked like a good way to build his career. Zac did not know, however, just how much of an impact the musical would have on his future.

Zac faced stiff competition for the **High School Musical** *movie.*

The opportunity to audition for the Disney Channel musical came just a few weeks after *Summerland* was cancelled. Zac felt his experience in musicals could help him to get a role in the production. But first he had to get an audition. Zac was not invited to audition, but he asked his agent to try to get him a casting call. Because the role involved singing and dancing, Zac thought he had a chance, and his agent was able to secure an audition for him.

Once he was there, Zac faced stiff competition. Hundreds of young actors were auditioning, all hoping to get a role in the film. When Zac's turn came to perform before the director, however, it did not take long for him to make an impression. After he sang only two eight-counts of a song he was asked to return for a callback audition. Zac had passed the first test.

Challenging Callback

Zac was still a long way from being part of the musical's cast, however. The callback audition proved to be much more difficult than his first audition. The number of people trying for the role of Troy Bolton had been narrowed down to fifteen, but there was still a long way to go.

For the audition Zac was paired with Vanessa Anne Hudgens. The sixteen-year-old with a sweet voice had made some guest appearances on children's television programs such as *The Suite Life of Zack and Cody* and *Drake and Josh*. As the audition progressed, Zac and Vanessa got to know each other and became comfortable performing together. They established a chemistry that the director began to notice. When there were about ten people left at the audition for both roles, the director began pairing the various actors and actresses in different ways. Zac and Vanessa remained a couple throughout the whole process, and they were not sure what this meant. "At the time we didn't know if it was chemistry or if they didn't like us or what was going on," Zac said.[26]

Neither Zac nor Vanessa was calm and collected during the audition. They were both nervous—too nervous to realize how

Musical Background

Zac wasn't the only *High School Musical* star to have a background in musical theater. His costar Vanessa Anne Hudgens got her start appearing in local musicals as well. When Vanessa was young, she had roles in community theater productions of musicals such as *The King and I, The Music Man,* and *The Wizard of Oz.*

well they clicked onscreen. Their lack of self-confidence actually helped them during the audition, Zac said. "I think that the people that did ... think they were great, were the ones that immediately got let go because they were so over-confident. It was the nerves that actually saved you."[27]

A Variety of Skills

The seven-hour audition included dancing, singing, and acting, as well as basketball skills. When a young actor was no longer needed, he was tapped on the shoulder. Some of the young actors found the audition process so demanding that they fainted.

Zac and Vanessa persevered. Zac found it helpful that he was a fan of musicals, such as *Grease* and *Singing in the Rain.* His experience in community theater also prepared him for the singing and dancing the role required.

In addition to singing and acting, however, the audition also called for him to show his basketball skills. This was by far his weakest area. One of the reasons Zac had become interested in acting was because sports were not his strong point. He could not avoid it now, however. Zac picked up a basketball and did what he could during the audition. While he was far from looking like a basketball superstar, he did well enough to pass.

Although Zac was not normally a jock, his role required him to learn how to play basketball well.

Immediate Connection

Actress Vanessa Anne Hudgens was paired with Zac during the auditions for *High School Musical* and right away she felt that the pair had chemistry. "The second I met him I thought he was a really cool guy," she said. "It's hard not to have chemistry with someone who is quite attractive."

"Teen Talks to: Zac Efron + Vanessa Hudgens," *Teen Magazine*, http://www.teenmag. com/celeb-stuff/zac-efron-vanessa-hudgens.

After a long day at the audition, Zac faced an even longer wait to find out if he got the part. It was a week and a half before he got the good news: He had won the part of Troy Bolton. Zac would have the lead role in the musical production, playing a high school basketball superstar who found he had a love for singing. Playing opposite him would be his audition partner, Vanessa. Being together throughout the audition process allowed them to get to know each other and build a chemistry that helped them to win the role.

Intimidating Role

Now that Zac had the part, the work began. His role called for him to dance, sing, and play basketball. In addition, he had to learn his lines and act. Zac had the male lead in the show and a great deal to learn.

The plot of *High School Musical* was a simple one. Troy and Gabriella, played by Zac and Vanessa, meet at a ski resort party where they find they both enjoy singing. Later they're surprised to discover they attend the same high school. They decide to audition for the school's musical but are held back by their friends who do not want them to leave their social circles. Troy is the

The roles of Troy and Gabriella were played by Zac and Vanessa Anne Hudgens.

Sharpay and Ryan were played by Ashley Tisdale and Lucas Grabeel.

Kiss that Wasn't

No kiss between Gabriella and Troy is shown in *High School Musical,* but one was filmed. The pair were not supposed to kiss, but Corbin missed a queue and by the time he arrived to break up the kiss, it had already happened. The clip shown in the movie, however, does not show Gabriella and Troy kissing.

star of the basketball team and is also pressured by his coach and father to spend time on the sport. Gabriella is a top student who is on the scholastic decathlon team. The team wants her to concentrate on math equations, not performing.

Adding another complication to the plot is another pair of students who want to star in the musical. Sharpay and Ryan Evans, played by Ashley Tisdale and Lucas Grabeel, also plot to prevent Troy and Gabriella from auditioning. They play a sister and brother who are used to having the leading roles to themselves.

The movie's plot was designed to appeal to teens who are figuring out where they fit in. Troy and Gabriella have to decide whether to follow their dreams or stick with things the way they are. Along the way, a romance develops between the two.

Extra Dancers

Turning the plot into a successful musical was not easy. *High School Musical* involved music, dance, and basketball sequences, sometimes all at once. The film needed a large cast of dancers and a number of synchronized moves. The movie was shot in Utah, and the best young dancers in the state were brought in as extras. Zac had experience in musicals but admitted that he was not the best dancer. He had to work hard to keep up with the

The other dancers were so good that Zac worked hard to get to their level.

talented young performers who were brought in for the movie's massive dance sequences.

At first, Zac was intimidated by the other dancers' talent. His lack of dance experience showed, but he had to put his worries to one side and get to work. "The only time I felt self-conscious during HSM was in the dances," he said. "I was always ten steps behind. So eventually I just put in the extra hours and forced myself to get better."[28]

High School Musical *got the best young dancers in Utah.*

Tiring Rehearsals

Zac knew he had a lot of work ahead of him in a short amount of time. The cast spent two weeks rehearsing in California and then filmed on location at a high school in Utah for four weeks. When he was rehearsing, his days began at 9 A.M. and ended at 5 P.M. Acting, dancing, and basketball were all part of Zac's schedule. The basketball and dancing he needed to do made his days tiring. After days of physically demanding rehearsals, Zac was achy and tired. "I got twisted ankles, shin splints and got all beaten up—but it was all for a good cause," he said.[29]

Playing basketball was another challenge for the young actor, who had always preferred theater to team sports. Zac had played basketball for a season when he was younger, but had felt like everyone else on the team was better than he was. "It was embarrassing," he said. "I think I scored two points all season. So, it took a lot of practice to say the least."[30]

To make it look like he knew what he was doing on the basketball court, Zac practiced for three hours each day. The practices were similar to those a real high school team would use. "We had to run suicides and get in the lay-up lines and we'd run several drills," he said. "At the end of the day, I just remember being so beat and beyond tired. I reached a new level of sleep every night. It was crazy."[31]

Stepping into the Role

The part of his job Zac felt most comfortable with was the acting. Once filming began, his talent began to show. Zac and Vanessa felt comfortable together during rehearsals, and that same connection came across in their scenes together.

Zac began to take on a different personality when he acted his scenes as Troy Bolton. He realized that he did not share many similarities with his character. Troy was a star athlete, a popular student, and a wonderful singer. The movie characterized him as such an all-around great kid that even Zac was in awe of the character he portrayed. "Troy's the cool kid," he said. "He has a magnetism I didn't possess in high school."[32]

Miscues

Not everything went perfectly when the cast was making *High School Musical*. In one scene, Zac had to run into the gym as he was putting on his shirt. He had to do the scene over and over when his microphone kept falling out of his shirt.

The actors in the show used humor to keep everyone sharp. At one point, Zac was too tired to smile for a reaction shot, so Vanessa switched places with an assistant director who was large and African American. When Zac looked back he saw the assistant when he expected Vanessa, and he could not help but laugh.

The hard work Zac put into his role did make him see one thing he had in common with his character, however. Troy's attitude was not completely different from Zac's. "I was not the most popular guy in school and I most certainly am not a star jock," he said. "However, we both work hard to accomplish our goals."[33]

All in This Together

To successfully play his part, Zac had to listen carefully to his dance instructor, basketball coach, and director. Making the movie wasn't simply about following directions, however. The film's director, Kenny Ortega, also encouraged input from the actors.

Ortega had also directed the 1987 film *Dirty Dancing* and was a director for television shows such as *Gilmore Girls*. He had learned about musical choreography from dance legend Gene Kelly and had worked with singers Madonna, Cher, and Gloria Estefan. The experienced director and choreographer knew what it was like to work with young actors and encouraged them to do what felt natural for their characters. The kids in the movie

Director Kenny Ortega encouraged the young actors' input.

had an idea of how they would respond in certain situations, and he listened to their advice. When the characters were having a conversation, he let them contribute about how they would really talk. He also listened to their ideas about the dance moves.

Ortega worked hard to create an atmosphere that pulled the cast together. He wanted the movie to look like the kids were really having fun, and he thought that the best way to do this was to have the kids in the cast enjoy themselves. To get everyone to work together, he created Teen Club Night. After filming was over for the day, the cast members could get together and just have a good time. "I think that's why the experience was so amazing," Zac's costar Ashley Tisdale said, "and maybe why this movie has become so successful because they saw how much fun we were having."[34]

In the evening, the actors would hang out together. Sometimes a group of them would go out to eat or head to the movies. They remained close throughout the making of the film. No romances began, they said, but a number of close friendships developed. "My favorite part of filming this movie was just the interaction with the cast, and making a whole bunch of new friends and singing and dancing while we were filming," Zac said.[35]

A Tight Schedule

The cast had to work hard in order to complete filming on the tight twenty-eight-day schedule, but Ortega was able to make the experience an enjoyable one. The director sometimes worried more about the cast having fun than he did about the movie he was making. His concerns led to the cast members pulling together and helping each other over the rough spots. "These kids were so 'there' for each other," Ortega said. "Some of them missed basketball practice so they could be on the sets to cheer on fellow actors doing practice runs."[36]

Zac was amazed by how much he was learning from the experience. It was hard for him to recall one part of the movie that stood out from the rest. "There were so many stand-out moments," he said. "We'd be working on a dance number with confetti shooting out at us—you don't get to do that every day. And we learned something new every day. Kenny would teach us all something."[37]

The bonding and friendship that grew in the cast while they were making the movie came across onscreen. The actors showed genuine happiness and enthusiasm in what they were doing. They were not only doing the required dance moves together, they all shared the same spirit. This type of togetherness was really obvious in the movie's final scene that has the cast singing "We're All in This Together" on the basketball court. "It was phenomenal, there was a strange elated feeling and I think we were all sharing it," Zac said. "It was a huge bonding moment and at the end of the night it was like magic was taking place."[38]

A Sour Note

Zac enjoyed the time he had spent making the movie. His acting had gone well and with effort he managed to pull off the dancing and basketball required for his role. However, there was one aspect of his role that he could not pull off himself. His singing did not blend well with the voices of the other members of the cast. To solve this problem, Drew Seeley was brought in to sing most of Zac's lyrics.

Zac's voice was changing as the movie was being made. The change became noticeable when he sang, because he could not hit all the notes. Because of this, Zac's voice was only used for the beginning and ending sections of his songs. Seeley did the rest of the singing. Zac received credit for singing some of the songs, but Seeley's name was also mentioned.

Moving On

The fact that Zac did not do much of his own singing in the movie did not appear to bother him. Zac had enjoyed making the movie, came away from the experience with new friends, and learned some new skills. He was a much better dancer and basketball player than he had been before starting to make the film. He also showed that he had a strong on-screen presence with his leading role.

The worst part of finishing the movie was leaving the friends he had made. "We became fast friends, and when it was over, everyone was devastated," he said. "It was so hard not to be able to go to the hotel room next door and knock. I made a lot of good friends, and we see each other all the time. If I could go back and do it again I'd do it in a heartbeat."[39]

Making the movie had been a great experience for Zac, but he had no idea just how the film would be received. Getting the part for *High School Musical* had meant dealing with a long audition process. After Zac got the role, there was the hard work that came with it. Making the movie was a difficult process, in which Zac had to develop his skills as an actor, dancer, singer, and basketball player. Now his job was complete. He thought he had made a little movie for the Disney Channel, and was ready to move on with his career.

However, Zac's life after *High School Musical* would be quite different from the one he had led before its debut, however. He came away from the film with the sense of a job well done, but would be rewarded with recognition that vastly exceeded his expectations. Before the musical's debut he was no different than thousands of kids with acting aspirations, hoping to get a break. After wrapping up the production of *High School Musical*, he didn't realize that he just had.

Chapter 4

High School Phenomenon

Zac did not realize it while he was making the movie, but getting cast as Troy Bolton in *High School Musical* would be his lucky break. Zac was honored to be cast in the movie, and enjoyed making it. However, he did not expect it to be more popular than any other television movie shown on the Disney Channel.

Zac and the other cast members were in for a surprise. The buzz about the movie began growing even before it was shown. *High School Musical* was becoming very popular with kids.

Impressive Premiere

Programming executives at the Disney Channel did not make the first showing of *High School Musical* a secret. Weeks before it was shown, the channel began doing some clever advertising for the show. Video clips from the movie and behind-the-scenes footage were shown to Disney Channel audiences in advance of the first screening.

Cast members began making live television appearances to promote the show as well. They were featured on a New Year's Eve special on the Disney Channel. A soundtrack of the show's songs was also made, and was released a week and a half before the movie first aired. Kids knew the movie was coming and were ready to watch.

High School Musical was first shown on January 20, 2006. The preview clips, videos. and songs had certainly captured

High School Musical *started becoming popular even before it was released.*

the interest of its audience. Kids tuned in and the movie's premiere set a network record with an average of 7.7 million viewers. It was the top-rated nonsports cable broadcast for the month.

It was not just the show that generated interest, however. The music from *High School Musical* was also popular. Kids could go to the Disney Channel Web site to download the lyrics to its songs. Within twenty-four hours of the show's premiere, the Web site got 1.2 million viewers and 500,000 downloads.

Zac said the show's popularity was because of its wholesome content. It had a story parents and kids could watch together without any uncomfortable moments. The fact that the show was a musical also set it apart from other teen movies, which typically did not include big song and dance numbers or love songs sung by the main characters. Zac, a fan of musicals, hoped

Musical would be the start of a new trend. He realized that the show's big production numbers, which included a large number of cast members dancing together, appealed to kids. "I expected, when I started, that hopefully we could bring musicals back into the spotlight," he said. "I grew up with a lot of musicals, it's all I watched. It's awesome to be able to bring a little bit of that back to Disney Channel."[40]

Mixed Reviews

Although kids enjoyed the movie a great deal, not all comments about the film were positive. Some reviewers looked at the show with a critical eye and did not see anything good about its simple message, good-looking characters, and catchy songs. Reviewer David Nair doubted that anyone besides young girls would enjoy the movie. … although the movie is mindlessly engaging for a while, the whole thing ultimately becomes so overwhelmingly silly and juvenile, it's difficult to imagine even the most die-hard fan of musicals finding anything here worth embracing," Nair said.[41] Marilyn Moss of HollywoodReporter.com found the musical to have a stale plot and a thin script. "The music and choreography were not enough to save it from a story that had been done before," she said. "Despite its upbeat premise … the Disney Channel original movie has about as much personality as the stale air that tries to inflate it and pump up its volumes," she said. "It's got plenty of musical numbers but never makes the grade to be an all-out, rollicking good time. It's hardly even a whimper."[42]

Other critics were more upbeat about the story and the way it was told. They found more to like about the show. The show's energetic dance numbers, talented cast, and engaging story pleased some reviewers. "It's doubtful that show tunes will ever be cool among teens and tweens, but Disney Channel certainly makes a convincing case for the return of the musical with an original pic from *Dirty Dancing's* Kenny Ortega," wrote reviewer Laura Fries in *Variety*. "Featuring an immensely appealing cast and some highly clever, toe-tapping

Surprise Hit

Executive Gary Marsh of Disney Channel Worldwide credited the connection between kids' real-life anxieties and the upbeat attitude of *High School Musical* as one reason for the show's success. Some called the movie corny, but Marsh saw it differently. "Kids' lives are awash in strife and stress, and this movie is optimistic, hopeful and celebratory," he said. "If being hopeful is corny, so be it. There's nothing wrong with being optimistic."

Misha Davenport, "Bop to the Top," *Chicago Sun-Times*, April 17, 2006.

tunes, *High School Musical* should strike the right chord with Mouse fans."[43]

A Hit with Kids

Young viewers did not pay much attention to what was being said about the movie. They were too busy watching it. The film did well with its target audience of kids age eight to eleven, who looked up to the high school students in the film. But it went beyond that—it appealed to teens as well. The movie was based on their social world and the love story between Troy and Gabriella, brought a touch of teenage romance. In addition, Zac's blue eyes appealed to young girls.

The movie had an overall appeal as well, with upbeat songs and dance numbers and a sports theme with a driving coach. Kids could also identify with the movie's message of being true to your own interests despite peer pressure. This combination created an entertaining film. "*High School Musical*, with its big throbbing heart, gives out all the right messages without being slow-witted or preachy," wrote reviewer Ken Tucker in *Entertainment Weekly*.[44]

Many products related to the show were developed, including books, games and dolls.

It seemed that kids could not get enough of the movie, and the Disney Channel kept showing different versions to hold their interest. At one point the movie was shown with lyrics printed on the bottom of the screen so kids could sing along. Another version had trivia and tidbits about the show pop up onto the screen. Still another taught kids the show's dance moves. *High School Musical* was shown six times between January 20 and February 13 and drew 26.3 million viewers.

A Wide Audience

In addition to being shown on television, a DVD version of the movie was also released. A remix version, with extra footage, was put out a few months later. Other products related to the show included books, dolls, and even a laundry hamper with a picture of the cast on the front. There was a *High School Musical* mystery date game, video games, and floor cushion. A play version of the musical was also developed so kids could stage their own version of the show, and a touring *High School Musical* ice show had skaters acting out the roles and doing its dance routines. "More than a TV movie and now more than a DVD, *High School Musical* is a phenomenon," wrote reviewer Ken Tucker in *Entertainment Weekly* magazine.[45]

It was not only in the United States that the movie was popular with young people. Recognition for the show grew worldwide when the movie was shown in foreign countries. The DVD version of the movie was also sold overseas. When *High School Musical* was released in the United Kingdom, it became the fastest-selling television film on DVD there.

The enormous success of *High School Musical* was much more than people had expected from the movie. Every time the musical was shown on television, its ratings improved. By the end of 2006, 12 million teens had seen the show. It won Emmy awards for outstanding children's program and outstanding choreography. It was also nominated in casting, directing, and original music and lyrics for "Get'cha Head in the Game" and "Breaking Free." The film became the highest-rated movie on the Disney Channel. "We never planned on this," said Gary Marsh of Disney Channel Worldwide. "This movie has taken on a life of its own."[46]

Popularity Surge

The show's cast members were as surprised as anyone by the film's success. They had enjoyed making the movie but had not realized how popular it would become. "We had no idea it was gonna blow up," said Vanessa.[47]

Gradually, the cast members began to learn just how much kids enjoyed the show. They were watching it, memorizing the songs and dance steps and putting themselves into the character's shoes. "It's so weird when people are like, do you understand that girls are having sleepovers and acting out the parts," said Ashley Tisdale. "And I'm like, you've gotta be kidding me. It's so crazy to think of, but I think this is so awesome."[48]

As the show's popularity began to build, Zac was careful not to get too carried away by the attention it brought. By late 2006, his

Punk'd with Ashley

After *High School Musical* became popular, Zac became a well-known enough celebrity to have a prank pulled on him for the television show *Punk'd*. Ashley Tisdale was in on the joke and went with him to a clothing store. While they were looking at the jeans, two people came in and took a box sitting on a table. When a manager came in and asked Zac about what had happened, Zac said the box had been taken, but the manager did not appear to believe his story. Zac was stunned by all the accusations going on around him, until Ashley finally let him in on the joke.

name was one of the most searched for on the Internet. However, Zac said he still thought of himself as an amateur. He was a high school kid and insisted that acting was more a hobby than a job for him. "At this point, when people ask me if I'm an actor, I say I'm a student," he said a few weeks after *High School Musical* premiered. "Acting has always been a hobby. It's just that now my hobby is taking off. My friends finally get to see what I've been doing all these years."[49]

Damage Control

The response to the movie was overwhelmingly positive. However, one of the few negative comments to come out of *High School Musical* was the fact that Zac did not sing all of his own songs. One of the reasons this became an issue was because the film's soundtrack was a surprising success. It rose to the top of the music charts, breaking into the top 10 in late January 2006. The album eventually went triple platinum and became the best-selling album of 2006 with 3.7 million copies sold in the U.S. *Breaking Free*, Zac's duet with his costar Vanessa Anne Hudgens, made it to No. 4 on Billboard's Hot 100.

Zac was listed as one of the performers of the song on the movie's soundtrack but how much singing he actually did on the song came into question. At first Zac did not talk about having his voice dubbed in the show's soundtrack, and instead expressed surprise at how popular it had become. "When you go on the Billboard chart, and you're looking at Mariah Carey, Kelly Clarkson and *High School Musical*. No way!" he said. "They have a typo right here."[50]

Recording Contracts

Zac's *High School Musical* costars Ashley Tisdale and Vanessa Anne Hudgens both signed record deals after the movie's soundtrack became popular. Zac was asked about that possibility for himself but said he was not sure if a CD was in his future. He blamed a lack of time for the project, saying he did not have time to do everything involved in creating a CD. If he would make a CD, he said, he wanted to do it right. "I wouldn't just have other people write songs and me go out and sing it," he said. "I would sit down with a guitar and write eleven or twelve good songs for an album and that is going to take a long time."[51]

The popularity of the *High School Musical* soundtrack led to a concert tour. The tour also promoted individual CDs made by members of the cast. Zac did not join the group on tour, however, because he was making another movie at the time. Instead, Drew Seeley, who had sung for Zac on the CD, went on the tour to do his vocals. Seeley was an Emmy Award-nominated singer and songwriter who co-wrote "Get'cha Head in the Game" for *Musical*.

Soon it became widely known that Zac had not done all of his own singing for the movie. When the news got out, Zac was relieved to talk about how his voice work was done. He admitted that his voice was changing at the time the songs for *High School Musical* were being recorded. He said Seeley's voice was blended with his to make it sound like he was hitting the high notes. The issue died down, and Zac said he planned to do his own singing in musicals he would make in the future.

Big Zac Attack

The news surrounding his singing for *High School Musical* had little impact on the attention Zac received from fans. He had got his first experience of fame after his work on *Summerland*, but the attention became much more intense after *High School Musical* premiered. Fans wanted to get in touch with Zac and found out how to do it. After the movie was shown on television, his family had to change their phone number at their home in Arroyo Grande. Fans had begun calling their home and asking for Zac. "Somehow our phone number got out online, and it got really bad," Zac said. "We were getting calls in the wee hours of the morning."[52]

Costars Ashley Tisdale (above) and Vanessa Anne Hudgens both signed record contracts after the movie.

Zac and the other cast members of **High School Musical** *signed autographs for thousands of fans.*

Now it was not only young girls who spotted Zac at the mall. He was often approached by strangers of all ages, boys as well as girls. Girls sang songs from the movie to him, such as "Breaking Free." Boys usually wanted to know if he was dating anyone in the cast. The musical had turned Zac from a budding actor into a star.

Star Treatment

The musical's popularity gave Zac the opportunity to be treated like a celebrity. When the DVD was launched in May 2006, a red-carpet Hollywood party was hosted by Buena Vista Home Entertainment. There were hundreds of fans there. They wanted autographs and pictures of Zac and the other members of the cast.

Zac also began going to awards shows. At the Teen Choice Awards, he won an award for Choice Breakout Star in the television category. Along with his musical costar Hudgens, he also won the Choice Chemistry award in the television category. *High School Musical* was a winner as well, taking the Choice Comedy/Musical Show award in the television category.

Zac was noticed for more than just winning awards, however. *Teen People* said he was one of the best-dressed stars at the ceremony. Zac was excited by the attention but tried not to get carried away by the publicity he was receiving. Other than signing many more autographs than he used to, he said his

Rising Stars

It wasn't only the stars of *High School Musical* who benefited from the success of the movie. Publications aimed at teens and tweens saw their sales go up when they featured the stars on the cover. Magazines such as *J-14, Twist, M, Tiger Beat, Bop,* and *Popstar* regularly included articles, photos, and posters about Zac, Vanessa Anne Hudgens, and Ashley Tisdale. The stars gave the publication quite a boost. "Some tween magazines say they have seen circulation rise by as much as 25 percent on the strength of 'High School Musical,'" journalist Elizabeth Olson noted.

Elizabeth Olson, "OMG! Cute Boys, Kissing Tips and Lots of Pics, as Magazines Find a Niche," *New York Times*, May 28, 2007 p. C1.

At the 2006 Teen Choice Awards, Zac (shown here with Paula Abdul) and High School Musical were both winners.

life was much the same. "I just can't get caught up in it," he said. "Otherwise I won't stay focused. It's very awesome. It's exciting."[53]

Dealing with Fame

The increased recognition Zac received was thrilling, but it also became a challenge for him. He was used to being recognized on occasion, but now he had to get used to living with even less privacy. When he went out in public, he was often noticed by fans.

Becoming a star meant becoming recognized and signing autographs.

Zac tried to sign autographs for his fans, but he found that this sometimes brought trouble. So many kids wanted an autograph that it sometimes became difficult for him to get away from a crowd. Once, when he went to a record store in a mall, a group of girls were lining up for a different record signing. When Zac walked into the store they noticed him. "The room went silent and all the little girls started pointing at me," he said. "I had to back up and run to my car."[54]

Another time, Zac went to a Cheetah Girls concert and agreed to sign an autograph for a little girl. Soon others were asking for an autograph, too. Pretty soon it seemed as if the whole audience wanted his autograph. It became such a distraction that security took Zac out of the building, and he had to wait outside until the concert started. Zac wasn't the only cast member to be noticed by the crowd. "Pretty soon my good friend Ashley Tisdale was thrown out there with me," he said.[55]

Rumors

Zac continued to remain friends with the other cast members from the movie. It turned out that when the movie finished, it was just the beginning of the time they would spend together. The cast traveled around the world to promote the movie, heading to London, Australia, and New York. They did interviews as a group. Soon there were plans in the works for a sequel.

All the time Zac was spending with the other cast members led to some rumors of romance. After he appeared in an episode of the Disney Channel show *The Suite Life of Zack and Cody*, there were rumors that he was romantically involved with Ashley Tisdale. Ashley was a regular on the show, and Zac appeared as a boy she had a crush on. Their romance was only part of the script, however, and they denied that there was anything romantic between them in real life. They told fans that they were just friends. "We just laugh every time we hear it," Zac said. "She's very cool. We hang out all the time. We're definitely not dating."[56]

Zac also appeared in a video for his costar Vanessa Anne Hudgens. In the video for her song *Say OK*, Zac played her

The cast members (here, Lucas Grabeel with Monique Coleman and Ashley Tisdale) of **High School Musical** *spent time together off the set.*

boyfriend and they were shown running around at a beach playground. Rumors started that they were dating, but both said little about their relationship other than to assure people they were good friends.

Going His Own Way

Zac had other things on his mind besides romance after making *High School Musical*. The musical had become a must-see show for teens and tweens and its popularity boosted his career. The show's success turned its stars, including Zac, into household names.

When he was cast in the role of Troy Bolton, Zac thought he would be making a minor musical for the Disney Channel. Now he had to decide what to do with the recognition and fame the show was bringing him. In some respects, Zac's career was going down a different path than that of his costars. When the other cast members went on a singing tour to promote their new albums and the musical, Zac continued to focus on the acting side of his career. Rather than recording an album, Zac moved on to another movie project. *High School Musical* had given him a new level of recognition, and he was going to do his best to take advantage of the opportunities it brought him.

Chapter 5

Beyond *Musical*

The success of *High School Musical* gave Zac the publicity he needed to build his career. He moved quickly from television to a major motion picture with big-name stars. Zac did not give up on the part that had brought him fame, however. He continued to do work for the Disney Channel and gladly appeared in a sequel to *High School Musical*. Zac also thought beyond his immediate opportunities. He looked forward to learning more about moviemaking in college and hoped to eventually work behind the camera.

As the popularity of *High School Muscial* grew, so did Zac's fame. The memorabilia in his family's home reflected his success. His father collected a stack of newspaper clippings and teen magazines that referred to Zac and he had a collection of *High School Musical* posters. Everywhere he looked, Zac saw proof that he had gone from hopeful teen actor to budding star.

In addition, new scripts were arriving. The fame Zac received from *Musical* was bringing him more choices. Zac had been used to being one of many actors trying out for a role. Now he had to decide whether or not to accept a role in a movie for the *Lifetime* network. He was also offered the opportunity to make a pilot for the Fox television network. There was so much going on all the time that Zac said he sometimes missed the simplicity of his pre-*Musical* life.

Keeping His Head

The increased attention would make it easy for fame to go to Zac's head, but he said his hometown friends kept him grounded. "I'm lucky enough to have friends that are so far removed from the industry that they do not care," he said. "I come home, and it's a reality check."[57]

Some aspects of Zac's life mirrored that of a typical teen. He still liked to play golf, ski, and snowboard. Thanks to his role in *Summerland*, he also knew how to surf. Zac graduated from high school in 2006 and was accepted at a college. He planned to attend the University of Southern California and study film. His life had changed a great deal since he had applied to college, however. More acting offers were coming his way, and his career was blossoming. Zac realized, however, that his success was because of one role and that his life could be very different if things had not worked out for him. "The only thing that separates us from anyone else with this movie is one single audition," he said.

> I could have dropped the basketball in my audition, I could have messed up on a line, or not been paired up with Vanessa

Wish Come True

Zac did not do all of his own singing in *High School Musical*, but when it was time to please a young girl, he was more than happy to break into song. A twelve-year-old girl from Florida, Erika Rumore, wanted to meet Zac. Her request was granted by the Make-A-Wish Foundation, which grants wishes for young people with life-threatening illnesses.

Erika got to spend the day with Zac on the set of *Hairspray*. He was filming the movie in Toronto, Canada, and Erika and her mom watched as they sat in the visitor chairs. Zac came over to Erika and gave her a hug and then ate lunch with her. "I was so happy I could hardly eat," she said. Zac gave her a signed picture, and as they left he asked if there was anything more he could do for her. She asked him to sing "Breakin Free," which he did on the spot. "He was so sweet," Erika said. "This was the best time of my life."

Kewl, "A Wish Come True," Spring 2007, p. 5.

during the audition. All of us recognize that we're extremely lucky to be here.[58]

Zac had the same interests as other teens, but the success of *Musical* meant that his life was far from ordinary. Zac's appeal to young audiences had been proven and he continued to do some work that was aimed at tweens and teens. He did voice work for the animated show *The Replacements*, in which he played a cartoon lifeguard named Davey Hunkeroff. He also appeared in several episodes of the Disney Channel show *The Suite Life of Zack and Cody* and appeared as himself on *The Disney Channel Games*.

In addition, *High School Musical* had been so popular that a sequel was planned. The cast would reunite to produce another film. Zac could not pass up this opportunity to work with his friends again and recreate the role that had made him a star. He gladly signed on to the project.

Next Level

Zac's fame gave him other options as well. He did not want to only be seen as a TV movie star. Zac was popular with young audiences, but he did not want to limit himself. To help expand his career, Zac signed with Creative Artists Agency in early 2007. The company was one of the top talent agencies in Hollywood. The success of *Musical* and his popularity with teens meant that Zac was now associated with a higher level of talent. Working with the agency could bring bigger movies his way.

Some scripts were offered to Zac, but he decided not to sit back and wait for work to come to him. Even after making *Musical*, Zac continued to go on auditions. Things were different for him now when he walked into a room to try out for a part. He was no longer an unknown actor, but someone with a recognizable face and name. Zac saw this as a nice benefit for his career. "The best perk I think is that going to the audition room, the casting director is at least somewhat familiar with your work, and that is always a big plus," he said.[59]

Hairspray

Zac's role in the supremely successful *High School Musical* was getting him noticed, but the squeaky clean nature of his character almost cost him his next role. A new, big-screen movie version of *Hairspray* was planned, and Zac wanted to try out for the role of television announcer Link Larkin. This movie would be a musical, but it had a very different tone than *High School Musical*. The film had big song and dance numbers, young stars, and a positive message, but it was aimed at an older audience. Zac had musical experience, but his innocent, youthful looks and previous work were quite different to the edgier style this role called for. When he auditioned for a role in *Hairspray* in summer 2006, director Adam Shankman said his image was "very Disney, very Mousketeery."[60]

Zac did not let this keep him from auditioning, however. He went up against 200 other young actors for one of the lead roles

Crazy Rumor

Zac's popularity meant that many stories were said about him, some true and some false. One time a friend called Zac to see if he was still alive, because he had seen some information online that said he had died.

Zac was indifferent when asked for his reaction to the rumor that he was dating his costar, Vanessa Anne Hudgens. "It's funny—they can say what they want," he said. "The same thing is said about me and Ashley and Vanessa and God knows who else. It's just funny that people are interested, and it goes back to the popularity of the movie." Vanessa Anne offered little more information. "We're such good friends, so to say that we're dating—I don't know. Rumors are rumors!"

"Teen Talks to: Zac Efron + Vanessa Hudgens," *Teen Magazine*, http://www.teenmag.com/celeb-stuff/zac-efron-vanessa-hudgens.

In auditioning for Hairspray, Zac had to prove himself to get the part.

Adoring Fan

Zac said his worst encounter with a fan happened when he was in a record store in Sherman Oaks, California. Zac was buying some dance DVDs for a friend when a girl recognized him and was stunned. "I was like 'Hey, how's it going?'" he recalled. "I was in the process of buying the DVDs so I'm giving money to the guy and she gives me a hug! Like a big ol' bear hug from behind. And I was sort of taken by surprise and I said, 'wow, thank you, that's awesome.'" The girl was not finished, however, and asked for a picture. Her friend took the picture, but as Zac was leaving, the girl came after him one more time. "She grabbed me, gave me another bear hug from the front and kissed me right on the side of the mouth," he said. Zac pulled away, but kept his cool. He left with a "I'll see you guys soon … catch you later," but was turned off by the overwhelming experience.

"Zac Efron's Freakiest Fan Encounter," *Teen Magazine*, http://www.teenmag.com/seen-in-teen/zac-efron-interview.

in the movie. Zac had several things to prove to the director. The first was that he was not an actor suited to just one type of role. Zac had to show that he could actually act in a way that was more outgoing than his everyday personality. Zac also had to show that he had an acting style that could appeal to adults as well, not just young girls or teens. In addition, Zac also needed to prove that he could handle the singing required by the role. Zac had not done all of his own songs in *High School Musical* and wanted to show that he could carry a tune.

Although Zac had a few hurdles to overcome in his audition, in his favor was his growing popularity. Zac's fame did not go unnoticed by the director. "He's a really special kid and is arguably the biggest teen star in America right now,"

Shankman said.[61] Zac realized that it was his role in *High School Musical* that got him considered for the part in *Hairspray*. He gave credit to the show for giving him the opportunity to have a chance at winning this role. "I guess you could say it's opened a lot of doors," he said.[62]

High Profile Film

Zac proved himself to the director, got the part, and began making a movie that was much bigger than anything he had done before. This big-budget motion picture had a number of experienced stars on board. Zac had previously worked with actors his own age who had some experience acting on television shows. They were all young actors who appealed to other kids.

The cast for the movie *Hairspray* would be quite different. Zac was very impressed to be sitting at a casting table with Christopher Walken, John Travolta, Michelle Pfeiffer, and Queen Latifah—all actors with extensive movie experience. Walken had won an Academy Award for best supporting actor for his dramatic role in *The Deer Hunter*, while Pfeiffer was an accomplished actress with films such as *Scarface* to her credit. Latifah, an outgoing rapper turned actress, had excelled in the movie version of the musical *Chicago*. In addition, child star Amanda Bynes was in the movie. Amanda had been the star of her own television show on the Nickelodeon channel and had the lead in teen-oriented movies such as *What a Girl Wants*.

But the actor who most impressed Zac was Travolta. He had also begun his career as a young actor, first gaining fame in the television series *Welcome Back Kotter*. Then came the dance-filled *Saturday Night Fever* and the popular musical *Grease*. With cutting-edge movies like *Pulp Fiction* Travolta had established himself as an acclaimed movie superstar. Working with Travolta and filming the movie with him in Canada was especially impressive for Zac. "He's such a legend," Zac said. "Just to meet him, I would have flown to Canada just to do that!"[63]

In Hairspray, Zac (far right) got to perform with some well-known actors, including Michelle Pfeiffer, Queen Latifah, John Travolta, Christopher Walken, and Allison Janney.

Newcomer Nikki Blonsky played the lead role of
Tracy Turnblad in **Hairspray.**

A Good Team

It wasn't only Zac who was impressed by the movie's cast. The first time the actors got together, director Adam Shankman looked around the room, saw all the talent, and was awed. Once rehearsals began and the actors began reading their lines, the dancers began dancing, the group began to click, and emotion filled the room. They were all feeling the excitement of the experience of creating the movie.

In addition to the experienced actors, there was a newcomer bringing a fresh outlook to the set. Nikki Blonsky would have the lead role of Tracy Turnblad and would be making her first movie. The eighteen-year-old had starred in musicals at her high school and was a *Hairspray* fan. It was a dream come true for her to be in the movie—she had been working in an ice cream shop when she tried out as part of a nationwide search and got the role. Blonsky was also awed by the amount of talent in the cast. "I'm just so thrilled," she said, soon after learning she landed the role. "I can't even begin to tell you everything that's running through my body."[64]

Accepting a Challenge

Once the talented cast was assembled, they began shooting the film. The preparation for *Hairspray* and the shooting schedule were much more intense than any acting project Zac had worked on before. It took much longer to make this big-screen movie than it had taken to make the other films Zac was used to. To prepare, Zac rehearsed for two months. He then spent four months shooting the picture. His character needed to be a leader, have charisma, and be somewhat of a rebel. In addition, Zac had to do some impressive dancing.

Zac was able to hold his own with his screen presence and deliver his lines but, once again, he found the dancing to be a challenge. The steps in *Hairspray* were more complicated than the ones he had to learn for *High School Musical* or the other stage musicals he had done. In his role as the show's master of

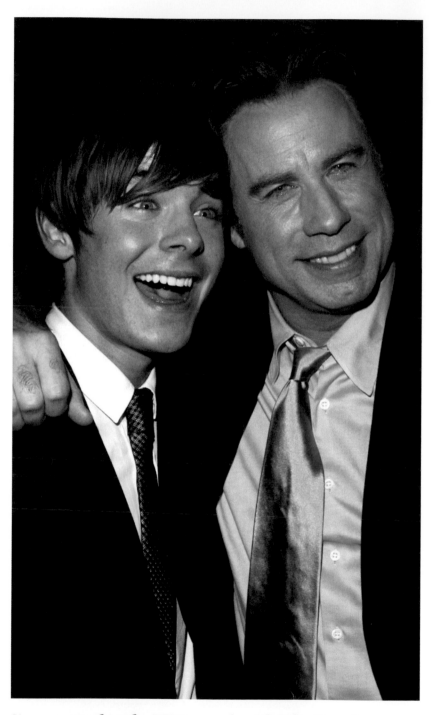

Zac appeared at the MTV awards with John Travolta.

ceremonies Link Larkin, Zac had to do dance steps similar to Elvis Presley's hip-shaking moves.

Zac also had some vocals to work on. In *Hairspray*, Zac hoped to put the issue of his singing in *High School Musical* to rest. He planned to do all of his own singing for *Hairspray*. Zac welcomed the chance to show how well he could sing. Doing his own singing for the movie would allow him to "regain some of my vocal dignity," he said.[65] To make the best use of Zac's singing style, the movie's songs were altered from the play version of the show. Instead of singing the ballad "It Takes Two," Zac was given a rock 'n roll song, "Ladies' Choice."

Heartfelt Film

Zac's character, Link Larkin, provided the romantic angle for the movie, because he fell for the lead character, Tracy Turnblad. The show revolved around Tracy's love of dancing and big hair. The plump, self-confident dancer's talent had earned her a spot on a television dance show. In addition, she stole Link's heart away from the show's star and competed for "The Miss Hairspray" title. Complications arose however, when Tracy found out about racial inequalities in her community, fought for integration, and had a run-in with the law. Like a true musical, the movie had a heartfelt message about not being afraid to have big dreams, or think that you have to fit in to succeed.

The movie was based on a Tony-award winning play, which had been based on a 1988 movie. The role of Tracy's mom, Edna, was traditionally played by a man dressed as a woman. In this movie version, Travolta had that role. Walken played Tracy's dad, and Bynes was her best friend, Penny Pingleton. Pfeiffer was Velma Von Tussle, the mother of Tracy's rival.

A Secondary Role

With all the stars in the movie and the addition of Blonsky, Zac was far from the star of the film. He had one of the principal roles, as a love interest for Tracy, but he was not the show's main

When Zac showed up at the MTV Awards in a gray Prada suit, one announcer said he deserved the best-dressed award.

Gangsta Chic

Announcer Coltrane said Zac deserved the best-dressed award when he showed up at the 2007 MTV Movie Awards in a gray Prada suit. Zac said deciding what to wear was actually a hassle, because he had to spend a whole morning deciding how to dress. One thing he decided not to wear, however, was socks. He said it was just too hot to bother with them.

character. Zac was a teen heartthrob, but the other stars in the cast were established and experienced actors. Much of the publicity for the film was centerd around Travolta playing a woman. In addition, when it came to stories about the movie's young stars, Blonsky had the freshest story and was the one who was most likely to be interviewed.

Zac's appearance in the movie was still an important moment, however. Being included in a film with established, experienced costars boosted Zac's career. While Zac was not always in the spotlight when the movie was publicized, he was always part of the crowd. And when the film was promoted to young audiences, Zac played a more important role. At the MTV movie awards a few months before the movie was released, it was Zac, along with Travolta and Bynes, who gave out an award. For his work in *Hairspray*, Zac received praise from director Shankman, who coached him to move away from his Disney style by turning down his smile. "Bigger things are waiting for him. He is a real actor, and he gives a real performance in this," he said.[66]

Back to School

When filming on *Hairspray* ended, Zac moved on to his next project; a sequel to *High School Musical*. The challenge for Zac and the entire cast was to re-capture the innocence and

All the stars of High School Musical signed up for the sequel.

excitement they had shown in the first movie. Zac's life had changed considerably since the film was released, and he now had to fall back into the character that had made him a star.

Although Zac had moved onto big-screen projects with major stars, he had no problem returning to the Disney Channel project. He said he was young for his age and did not mind being cast as a high schooler even though he had already graduated. After the success of *High School Musical*, Zac said he had his sights set higher than Disney Channel projects but realized he had nothing to lose by making a sequel that he knew would be popular with his fans. "High school is a defining point in your history," he said.

> Everyone remembers high school. At that age, there is so much drama and so many funny stories and great things happen. It shapes who you are. As long as we can portray this age group, I think I'm going to keep doing it.[67]

The other actors in the first *High School Musical* agreed, and they all returned for the second film. Director Kenny Ortega, who also choreographed the movie, said all of the cast members had a great attitude toward the sequel. Everyone felt they owed it to each other, and to the movie's fans, to come back. "People may have told them, 'You could move on to something bigger and better.' But what's bigger and better?" Ortega said.[68]

Once the actors got back to the set, they felt the same chemistry they had the first time around. The emotion and excitement of making the first movie returned. "It's been so much fun," Ortega said. "The team is back and more dedicated to making a great picture than ever."[69]

Musical Romance

High School Musical 2: Sing it All or Nothing had the same main characters as the first film but this time on summer vacation. The setting was a country club, where Troy worked as a lifeguard and

Gabriella was a waitress. When they planned to sing a duet at the country club talent show, Sharpay and Ryan, once again played by Ashley Tisdale and Lucas Grabeel, were determined to break them up in order to win the contest. Romance entered the picture again, when Sharpay pretends to drown so Troy would have to save her. Ryan used this moment to try to convince Gabriella that Troy was cheating on her with Sharpay.

The movie also featured musical numbers alongside the sport of baseball and let its characters grow and learn. "This movie is a little bit more emotional; it's a little deeper than the first one. The first movie really gave kids permission to feel like they could believe in their dreams and follow their heart," said Monique Coleman, who played Taylor McKessey, scholastic decathlon captain. "This go-around it really takes it to that next step and asks you to accept responsibility for the choices that you make."[70]

In addition to the romance between Troy and Gabriella, the movie also featured a budding relationship between Chad and Taylor, played by Corbin Bleu and Coleman. Bleu's character is only interested in basketball in the first movie, but he begins to see that there is life beyond the three-point line.

The interest in the romantic angle of the movie was enhanced by rumors that Zac and his costar, Vanessa Anne Hudgens, were indeed dating. When the *High School Musical* cast went to South America for a tour, Zac went along. He was not scheduled to sing,

Starstruck

Teen Magazine asked Zac who he would talk to if he could ask any celebrity a question. Zac chose Kobe Bryant. He would ask the Los Angeles Lakers star how he got so good at basketball.

Their Top Picks

Before *High School Musical 2* was released, several of the show's stars talked about their favorite songs in the movie. Ashley Tisdale, who played the mean Sharpay Evans in the film, liked the song "What Time Is It?" from the beginning of the movie. "It's just fun," she said. "It shows off all the characters, and you know what they're excited about for the summer."

Monique Coleman, who played decathlon team captain Taylor in the film, liked "Gotta Go My Own Way," a solo sung by Vanessa Anne Hudgens. "I love it, because I think it's kind of a girl-power song about really being an individual— realizing that sometimes in life, you have to choose yourself over choosing a relationship. It's a really sweet song, and she sings it beautifully."

For his favorite, Corbin Bleu, who played Chad in the musical, chose "I Don't Dance." The number was set on a baseball field. "It's a mixture, like a *West Side Story* kind of thing, because it's got the whole Sharks and Jets battle thing going on. And I just love the fact that it mixes the sport of baseball with the actual dancing."

Larry Carroll, "'High School Musical' Stars Dish on Sequel's Showstoppers, Love Triangles," MTV.com, June 6, 2007, http://www.mtv.com/movies/news/articles/1561761/story.jhtml.

but went along as a friend of Vanessa's. To prevent any questions about the quality of his voice, Zac did all of his own singing for the second *Musical*.

The show was again heavily promoted and expected a welcome reception by its fans. The Web site had a second-by-second countdown to the movie's August release. Months before it aired, commercials promoted the film as the start of something new. Tidbits about the making of the movie were included on the Disney program *Road to High School Musical 2*, which was shown weekly in the months leading up to the movie's premiere.

More to Come

There was no shortage of work for Zac after filming ended on *High School Musical 2*. Zac had promotional work to do for that movie, and for *Hairspray* as well. In addition, more acting offers were coming his way. While making *High School Musical 2*, Zac signed on as the star of a comedy in a high school setting written by Jason Filardi. The project had a *Hairspray* connection as well, as Adam Shankman, the movie's director, was one of the producers of the show, through Offspring Entertainment. Jason Barrett, Zac's manager, was the movie's executive producer.

There were also plans to make a third *High School Musical*, for release in theaters. The movie had made Zac a star and had the staying power to continue to help him move his career forward.

However, Zac knew he could not play a high school student forever. He was already thinking about what would happen after he outgrew teen roles. Zac hoped to take on roles that would be more mature, as his fans grew up as well. Zac did not mind doing young roles for the time being, but he thought about doing other things such as going into action films. "I would love to do edgier roles but it needs to be the right project with a good story," he said. "In a few years, when I do more adult projects, my fans also will be a little more mature so it'll be fun to grow up with the fans."[1]

Zac thought about working behind the camera as well. He had put off college for a year when he got the role in *Hairspray*,

Musical Perks

The cast of *High School Musical* got a nice present from Disney when the movie became a success. They were rewarded with 32-inch flat-screen TVs.

Zac Tidbits

Teen magazines were filled with information about Zac and other young stars. They offered insights and bits of information about their likes and dislikes. *Bop* magazine featured Zac on the cover with the question "Has fame changed Zac?" Inside, Zac revealed that his life had stayed much the same since *High School Musical* premiered. "I don't have a fancy car. I don't live in a mansion," he said. However, he didsplash out on one hobby. He said the thing that he treasured most was his comic book collection.

The same issue featured another piece of information on the young star. It took only forty-five minutes from the time he woke up for him to be out the door, he said. "I can get ready pretty quickly," he said.

"Is Zac Still Down-to-Earth?" *Bop*, April 2007, p. 10.

but he still planned to continue with his schooling. Working as a producer or director one day was a possibility for the budding star. With *High School Musical* on his résumé, and the talent and drive to continue his career, Zac's future was a promising one.

Chapter 1: He'd Rather Act

1. "Ashley and Zac Talk Back," *Newsweek*, July 24, 2006, http://www.msnbc.msn.com/id/14015421/site/newsweek.
2. Stacy Jenel Smith, "Zac Efron's Summerland Transformation," http://zacefronfan.org/press/transformation.php.
3. "Summer Guy," http://zacefronfan.org/press/summerguy.php.
4. Patrick S. Pemberton, "He acts, he sings—and he's local," *San Luis Obispo Tribune*, http://zacefronfan.org/press/local.php.
5. "Q and A with Teen Hollywood," http://zacefronfan.org/press/qahollywood.php.
6. Patrick S. Pemberton, "He acts, he sings—and he's local," *San Luis Obispo Tribune*, http://zacefronfan.org/press/local.php.
7. Patrick S. Pemberton, "He acts, he sings—and he's local," *San Luis Obispo Tribune*, http://zacefronfan.org/press/local.php.
8. "Behind the scenes of High School Musical," *Scholastic News*, http://zacefronfan.org/press/behindsceneshsm.php.

Chapter 2: Teen Dream

9. "The Art of Being: Introducing Zac Efron," TheWB.com, http://zacefronfan.org/press/intozac.php.
10. "Zac Efron 'in the spotlight,'" http://zacefronfan.org/press/spotlight.php.
11. "The Art of Being: Introducing Zac Efron," TheWB.com, http://zacefronfan.org/press/intozac.php.
12. Stacy Jenel Smith, "Zac Efron's Summerland Transformation," http://zacefronfan.org/press/transformation.php.
13. "Zac Efron 'in the spotlight,'" http://zacefronfan.org/press/spotlight.php.
14. "Zac Efron 'in the spotlight,'" http://zacefronfan.org/press/spotlight.php.
15. "Zac Efron 'in the spotlight,'" http://zacefronfan.org/press/spotlight.php.

16. "Summer Guy," http://zacefronfan.org/press/summerguy.php.
17. Stacy Jenel Smith, "Zac Efron's Summerland Transformation," http://zacefronfan.org/press/transformation.php.
18. Aidan Quinn Applauds work of Teens who play the autistic Teens, http://zacefronfan.org/press/aidanquinn.php.
19. The Derby Stallion, "Zac Interviews, View #3," http://www.thederbystallion.com/index.html.
20. The Derby Stallion, "Zac Interviews, View #3," http://www.thederbystallion.com/index.html.
21. The Derby Stallion, "Zac Interviews, View #2," http://www.thederbystallion.com/index.html.
22. David Cornelius, "The Derby Stallion," DVD Talk, June 4, 2007, http://www.dvdtalk.com/reviews/review.php?ID=28432.
23. Francine Brokaw, "The Derby Stallion," MovieWeb, http://www.movieweb.com/dvd/release/73/122073/review2470.php.
24. Patrick S. Pemberton, "He acts, he sings—and he's local," *San Luis Obispo Tribune*, http://zacefronfan.org/press/local.php.
25. David Cornelius, "The Derby Stallion," DVD Talk, June 4, 2007, http://www.dvdtalk.com/reviews/review.php?ID=28432.

Chapter 3: Making *Musical*

26. "Teen Talks to: Zac Efron + Vanessa Hudgens," *Teen Magazine*, http://www.teenmag.com/celeb-stuff/zac-efron-vanessa-hudgens.
27. "Zac Efron, Vanessa Anne Hudgens: High School Musical," Teen Television, http://zacefronfan.org/press/zacvanessa.php.
28. "Ashley and Zac Talk Back," *Newsweek*, July 24, 2006, http://www.msnbc.msn.com/id/14015421/site/newsweek.
29. Dallas Morning News, "Learning to be 'High School' stars," http://zacefronfan.org/press/learninghstars.php.
30. "Zac Efron, Vanessa Anne Hudgens: High School Musical," Teen Television, http://zacefronfan.org/press/zacvanessa.php.
31. "Zac Efron, Vanessa Anne Hudgens: High School Musical," Teen Television, http://zacefronfan.org/press/zacvanessa.php.
32. Lindsay Soll, "Teen Choice 2006: Zac Attack," *Teen People*, September 2006, p. 64.

33. "Ashley and Zac Talk Back," *Newsweek*, July 24, 2006, http://www.msnbc.msn.com/id/14015421/site/newsweek.

34. Hanh Nguyen, "'Musical' cast talks fame and future," May 23, 2006, www.zap2it.com/zap-highschoolmusicalcastfame future,0,834080.story.

35. Emily Doveala, "The Scoop on 'High School Musical,'" *Time for Kids*, http://zacefronfan.org/press/scoophsm.php.

36. M. D. Caprario, "'High School Musical' to Premiere on Disney Channel Weekend of January 20th," LASPLASH.com, http://www.lasplash.com/publish/cat_index_Entertainment_and_Culture/_High_School_Musical_to_Premiere_on_Disney_Channel_Weekend_of_January_20th.php.

37. M. D. Caprario, "'High School Musical' to Premiere on Disney Channel Weekend of January 20th," LASPLASH.com, http://www.lasplash.com/publish/cat_index_Entertainment_and_Culture/_High_School_Musical_to_Premiere_on_Disney_Channel_Weekend_of_January_20th.php.

38. Heather Keets Wright, "Have You Met Zac?" *TeenPeople.com*, February 10, 2006.

39. "Behind the Scenes of High School Musical," *Scholastic News Online*. http://zacefronfan.org/press/behindsceneshsm.php.

Chapter 4: *High School* Phenomenon

40. Emily Doveala, "The Scoop on 'High School Musical,'" *Time for Kids*, http://zacefronfan.org/press/scoophsm.php.

41. David Nair, "Six Disney Channel Original Movies," *Reel Film Reviews*, http://www.reelfilm.com/disorig.htm#high.

42. Marilyn Moss, "High School Musical," HollywoodReporter.com, http://hollywoodreporter.com/hr/search/article_display.jsp?vnu_content_id=1001881997.

43. Laura Fries, "High School Musical," *Variety*, January 18, 2006, http://www.variety.com/review/VE1117929285.html?categoryId=32&cs=1.

44. Ken Tucker, "Awake and Sing!" *Entertainment Weekly*, May 26, 2006.

45. Ken Tucker, "Awake and Sing!" *Entertainment Weekly*, May 26, 2006.

46. Misha Davenport, "Bop to the Top," *Chicago Sun-Times*, April 17, 2006.

47. "A Look at 'High School Musical,'" 7M Pictures, http://zacefronfan.org/press/lookhsm.php.

48. "A Look at 'High School Musical,'" 7M Pictures, http://zacefronfan.org/press/lookhsm.php.

49. Heather Keets Wright, "Admit It: You Saw *High School Musical*," *Teen People*, Feb. 10, 2006.

50. "A Look at 'High School Musical,'" 7M Pictures, http://zacefronfan.org/press/lookhsm.php.

51. "All New Q and A with Zac Efron," *Teen Magazine*, http://zacefronfan.org/press/newqa.php.

52. Patrick S. Pemberton, "He acts, he sings—and he's local," *San Luis Obispo Tribune*, http://zacefronfan.org/press/local.php.

53. "They Rock," http://zacefronfan.org/press/theyrock.php.

54. "Showy Success for Kids Musical," *Los Angeles Times*. February 27, 2006, p. E1.

55. "Who's that Babe?" *Teen Magazine*, http://zacefronfan.org/press/zacteenmagazine.php.

56. "A Look at 'High School Musical,'" 7M Pictures, http://zacefronfan.org/press/lookhsm.php.

Chapter 5: Beyond *Musical*

57. "A Look at 'High School Musical,'" 7M Pictures, http://zacefronfan.org/press/lookhsm.php.

58. "Teen Talks to: Zac Efron + Vanessa Hudgens," *Teen Magazine*, http://www.teenmag.com/celeb-stuff/zac-efron-vanessa-hudgens.

59. "'High School Musical' stars enjoy instant fame," *The Plain Dealer*, http://zacefronfan.org/press/hsmstantfame.php.

60. "'High School Musical' Star lands 'Hairspray' lead," June 26, 2006, www.tv.com.

61. Johnnie L. Roberts, "Hollywood: Hello to 'Hairspray,'" *Newsweek*, July 3, 2006, p. 14.

62. Lynette Rice, "The Cast of High School Musical," *Entertainment Weekly*, December 29, 2006, p. 80.

63. "High School Musical," Digital Spy, http://zacefronfan.org/press/hsmdigital.php.

64. "A Hairspray Dream Come True," MSNBC, June 15, 2006, http://www.msnbc.msn.com/id/13351480.

65. Johnnie L. Roberts, "Hollywood: Hello to 'Hairspray,'" *Newsweek*, July 3, 2006, p. 14.

66. Susan Wloszczyna, "Familiar Fare Freshens Up," USA Today, January 18, 2007, p. 8d.

67. "Zac Efron, Vanessa Anne Hudgens: High School Musical," Teen Television, http://zacefronfan.org/press/zacvanessa.php.

68. Debbie Hummel, "Team Spirit Renewed for 'High School Musical 2,'" Indystar.com, http://www.indystar.com/apps/pbcs.dll/article?AID=/20070510/ENTERTAINMENT05/705100314/1007/LIVING.

69. Debbie Hummel, "Team Spirit Renewed for 'High School Musical 2,'" Indystar.com, http://www.indystar.com/apps/pbcs.dll/article?AID=/20070510/ENTERTAINMENT05/705100314/1007/LIVING.

70. Larry Carroll, "'High School Musical' Stars Dish on Sequel's Showstoppers, Love Triangles," MTV.com, June 6, 2007, http://www.mtv.com/movies/news/articles/1561761/story.jhtml.

71. "Ashley and Zac Talk Back," *Newsweek*, July 24, 2006, http://www.msnbc.msn.com/id/14015421/site/newsweek.

1987

Zachary David Alexander Efron is born on October 18.

1998

Zac begins trying out for plays and lands a role in a community production of *Gypsy*.

2002

A small role in the television series *Firefly* gives Zac his first professional acting job.

2003

Zac gets a role in the television pilot *The Big Wide World of Carl Laemke*.

2004

A guest role on the television series *Summerland* goes to Zac. He also makes *Miracle Run*, his first television movie.

2005

Zac becomes part of the *Summerland* cast, but the series is cancelled. He gets his first lead movie role with *The Derby Stallion* and also gets the lead in *High School Musical*.

2006

High School Musical premieres and is a hit with teens and tweens, sending Zac's popularity soaring.

2007

Zac works with big-name stars on the motion picture *Hairspray*. He again steps into the role of Troy Bolton in *High School Musical 2*.

Books

Grace Norwich, *Zac Attack: An Unauthorized Biography*, New York: Penguin Group, 2006. This paperback looks at Zac's life and career and includes fast facts about the star.

Kathy Tracy, *Zac Efron*, Hockessin, Delaware: Mitchell Lane Publishers, 2007. This easy-to-read book contains information about Zac's life and career.

Web Sites

Entertainment Weekly (www.ew.com). Features the latest news about Zac and other celebrities.

Internet Movie Database (www.imdb.com). Get information on Zac's latest movies and a list of his film work.

People (www.people.com). A search for Zac Efron brings up news about the star.

TV.com (www.tv.com). Check out Zac's biography for his background and lots of trivia.

Terri Dougherty is a writer and reporter who enjoys learning new things every day and writing books for children. She lives in Appleton, Wisconsin, with her husband, Denis, and three children, Kyle, Rachel, and Emily. Terri and her daughters love to watch *High School Musical* and understand its appeal.